two at one piano

early intermediate duets
music by JON GEORGE

commissioned by Frances Clark
edited by Louise Goss

Contents

Cover Design: Candy Woolley

© 1976 Summy-Birchard Music
division of Summy-Birchard Inc.
All Rights Reserved   Printed in U.S.A.
Distributed Exclusively by Alfred Publishing Co., Inc.
ISBN 0-87487-143-3

Summy-Birchard Inc.
exclusively distributed by
Warner Bros. Publications
15800 NW 48th Avenue
Miami, Florida 33014

Ancient Procession

Secondo

With simple dignity

poco a poco crescendo al Fine

simile

molto rit.

Ancient Procession

Primo

On the Hacienda

Secondo

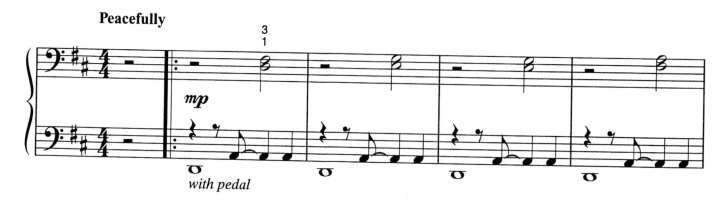

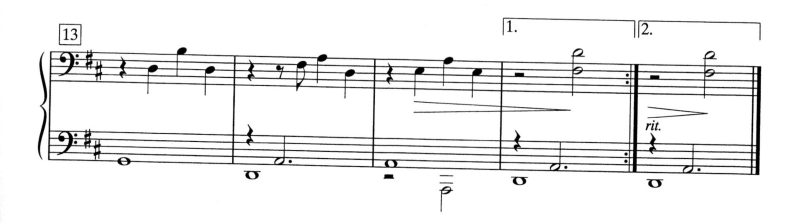

On the Hacienda

Primo

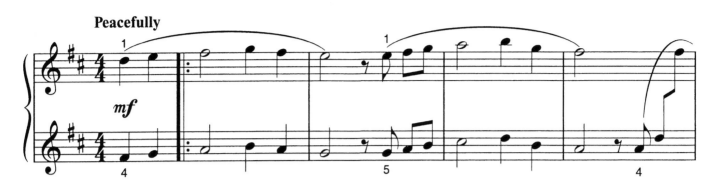

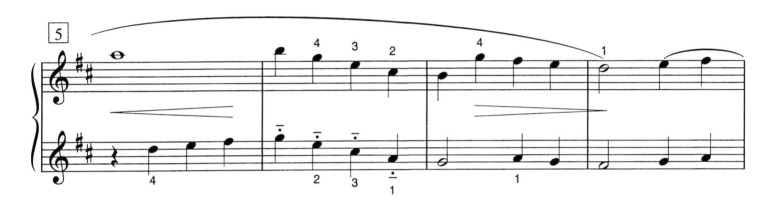

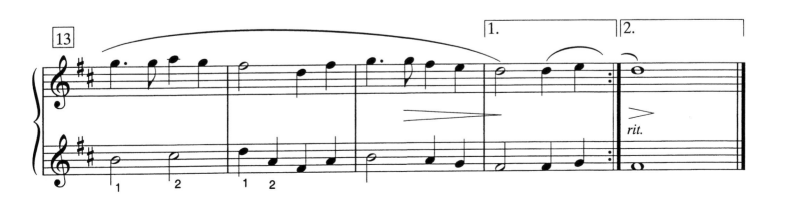

Village Dance

Secondo

Village Dance

Primo

Forest Flower

Secondo

Forest Flower

Primo

Trolley Song

Secondo

Trolley Song

Primo

Pastorale

Secondo

Pastorale

Primo

Celebration

Secondo

Celebration

Primo